knowledge Power Perseverance
ambition Faith Resilience
confidence Greatness Prestige

POETIQUE
SOUL

L.

L. Books

Atlanta, GA. 30314

Cover Illustration and Design: Phillip Davis

ISBN- 13: 978-0615987675
ISBN-I 0: 0615987672

Manufactured in the United States of America

Acknowledgements

First, I would like to thank God for blessings me with a love for words that allows me to express what I feel and see in myself and others through my writing. I find my inspiration in all sorts of things, situations, and people. I would also like to thank my mom and grandmothers for molding me into the strong minded, ambitious young woman I am today. Thanks to my sons for teaching me responsibility and discipline at a young age, and also for adding ammunition to my strong drive to succeed each day. I'm grateful for my dad setting the standards as to how every man should treat me and teaching me not to tolerate anything less. I would like to express my deepest gratitude to my sister Shaquita Newton, Thank you for being by my side to support me in anything I do including all of the effort put into this project. I would also like to say thanks for believing in me, you constantly spark my creativity and I love that about you. To my mentor Mrs. Cynthia Jenkins, thanks for always giving me words of wisdom and inspiration to allow me to open up my mind to a broader view of life. A special thanks to Mr. Phillip Davis for the illustration and design of my book cover, you really brought my vision to life and I appreciate it. Thank you to all of my family and friends for continuously supporting me on my journey.

To Life, I appreciate the obstacles and hurdles you have thrown my way. They could have broken me down completely, but instead they built me up even stronger than before. I would now like to present to you all *Poetique Soul*.

Much Love,

L.

Contents

Greatness

Why must I not be great?
Who says that I have to wait?
Tired of standing at a static door?
Then its time to open up my wings and soar.

Why stand in the shadows when I am the light?
Why pretend to lose when I've won that fight?
So caught up in everyone else's needs
That I haven't found time to plant my own seeds

Why not get up each time I fall down
I am a queen I deserve the crown.

Why not rise up and face my fears
They've disparaged me enough throughout the years.
Hold back for what, why not speak out
So what if they talk and cast their doubts

I was born to be a beautiful butterfly
Why stay a caterpillar, without wings I can't fly.
Why would I wither and refuse to grow
When I am a star, the leading lady of the show

I will persevere, I must succeed
Because I am a diamond, a very rare breed.

Know Who I Am

From this day forward
They will know who I am
I will be known as the virtuoso
That I truly I am
They will be inspired by my resilience
Intrigued by my brilliance
My Presence shall never be replaced
My essence will not be effaced
Creating my own propriety
Or must I acquiesce to society?
My self portrait I paint aesthetically
These words I speak prophetically
In the words of the late great Dr. King
I too have a dream
Of growing from just an ordinary girl
Into a woman of prestige

Authentic

I was cut from a different cloth
While you are all a part of the same old quilt
You are one of many
See me, I was custom built
Authenticity at its finest
Originality no denying
My inadequacies and insecurities
Are what makes me the perfect me
If they were never present
What would distinguish her from me?

My Sons

I love my sons with all of my heart
I knew this was true love right from the start
Whatever it takes to keep a smile on their face
Because they motivate me to keep running the race
Whether its ups or downs
Through smiles and frowns
I'll be by their side
Pick them up when they're down
Wipe tears from their eyes
And comfort their cries
When there is no other
They can depend on their mother
With God by my side
I will always provide
Do the best that I can
To raise boys into men
During tough times and all
I will be around
Because I am the foundation for their solid ground

This Place

Coming from a place where outside your door
There should be green grass
But there is red dirt
Looking into young eyes
Where there should be joy
There is a prevalent hurt
Feels like you're trapped inside
With no possible way out
Where you have big dreams
Everyone else has strong doubts
A place where guns are given to boys
As if they are toys
Where girls are having babies
Before they've been taught to be ladies
How can you expect a boy to be a dad?
When he never learned to be a man
In this place where the drugs outweigh the hugs
How do you find the strength to rise above?
No setting goals or reaching dreams

Blinded by the possession of material things
Confined to this place, its mentality, and everything in it
Ignorant to the fact that there is no limit
No limit to what or who you can be
Just open up your mind and set it free
Remember where you're from
But find where you're going
Remember every flower was once a seed
That eventually started growing

Think

A hard head

Makes a soft behind

You cannot get ahead

By following the blind

If you step in quick sand

Then you will sink

Before making choices

Be sure to think

My Struggle

You don't know my struggle
You don't know my pain
The only thing you know for sure is my name
You couldn't take a step in my shoes
You don't have the voice to sing my blues
Try keeping your head above water
As the currents get stronger
Try remaining patient
As the wait seems to get longer
You haven't endured the hungry nights
And still kept faith that the future is bright
Have you cried tears that lasted for years?
Jumped over hurdles
And kept running the race
With ambitions and hopes of still winning first place.

Stay Strong

How are you supposed to stay strong?
When the wait seems oh so long
It seems like the harder you try
The more tears you have to cry
How are you supposed to stay strong?
When everything around you seems to go wrong
Things start to look up, only to fall back down
It's like a cycle that keeps going around.
You try to be happy and hold back your tears
You even keep your head up and face all of your fears
This can't be life there has to be more
I guess it takes time to find the right door
Which is the door that leads to success?
There has to be an outlet from all of the stress
You have to weather the storm to get to the sunshine
But you've given it your all, when will it be your time?
There's only one thing that I know will work
Bowing your head with your knees in the dirt
God will make a way for you to succeed
All you have to do is pray
Prayer changes things!

Faith

Faith is seeing the sunlight
Through the storm and the rain
Faith gives you a reason to smile
Even in the midst of pain

Faith is walking through darkness
Knowing that you'll find the light
Faith is when you're down to your last
Still believing everything will be alright

Though you may be blind
With faith you shall see
Faith gives you the power to unlock
Without the master key.

Never Give Up

I was once terrified of the water
But then I learned to swim
I got fed up with losing
So I began to win
Became disgusted with the bottom
So I reached for the top
I made up my mind
I refused to be stopped
Overcome every obstacle
Break down every door
I will not be weary
And suffer anymore
With so much potential
Destined to be great
My impatience has grown I can no longer wait
The time has come
To share my gift with the world
There's much more to me
I'm not your average girl
With loads of ambition
A strong will of my own
I will not give up
Until I sit on the throne.

Reality

Why were some people born with silver spoons?
While we were born with plastic
Why were they given a head start?
While we're still stuck in traffic
Why is it that when we strive to do right
Wrong keeps being found
Why do we have to fight for royalty?
While their just handed the crown
Why is it so hard
When you've given it your all,
Your very best
Is this really life?
Or is this a test?
Can we really make it to the top?
Or is this our fate?
If we put our best foot forward
Will we still come in last place?
Maybe when we awake from this terrible nightmare
We'll open our eyes, and already be there
Is it all a bad dream?
Or just the reality of things

No Longer Bound

Being a victim of circumstance
Not even given a chance
To prove you are equal, if not a better man
Born with the odds against you
Not given a choice
Being forced to whisper
As if you have no voice
Made you think you were nobody
But you had to be somebody
Knew that if you realized you were somebody
Then they would be nobody
Being kept in the dark
For they were afraid of your light
Knew once it was lit
It could only shine bright
No longer lost
Awakened and found
Broken from bondage
And no longer bound
Now that you have a choice
Recognize your voice
Look up and be proud
You are no longer bound!

Fear vs. Faith

Fear is a liar
Faith is the truth
Fear is an impediment
While faith sees you through

Fear is inferior
Faith is superior
Fear holds you back
And faith draws you nearer

Fear cuts off your life line
Where faith gives you a lifetime
Fear remains at the end of the line
And faith turns water into wine.

Worthy

What is your purpose?
Is he really worth it?
He sits comfortably on a branch
While you go out on a limb
Seems as if he doesn't see the value in you
As you do in him
Why does he treat you bad?
And do the things he do
A man only goes as far
As you allow him to
Demand your respect
Or settle for less
Treat yourself as a queen
And watch everyone take heed
If he isn't there
Then why should you care
Open up your eyes
Stop playing blind
He isn't worthy of you
Or your precious time
Respect should be reciprocated
As loving gestures are appreciated.

Broken Heart

You try not to judge them all by one man's deceit
And you keep this in mind for the next man you meet
But how can you love again or even open your heart
When your feelings have been crushed
And it's broken from the start
Once your heart has been broken, it is hard to mend
Even more difficult to let another man in
He says that he's different, if you'd just give him a try
But you can't help but wonder
Would he lie and make you cry?
Would he cheat or would he fight?
Is he the type not to come home at night?
All of these questions and thoughts running through your head
You want to love again but being hurt is what you dread
Each time it's different or is it really the same?
In the beginning it's all good
And in the end it's all game
Tired of the strife
You make a vow to the single life

Since no man is worthy of you ever being his wife
Feels like there's this void that can't be filled
Where your heart has been broken
The scar still hasn't healed
Been looking for love in all the wrong places
Been searching for Mr. Right in all the wrong faces
There is this one guy who deserves your all
His name is Jesus just give him a call
Now close your eyes and begin to pray
No more looking for love
He'll send love your way

Live and Learn

You suffer in silence
You weep in private
In their eyes you're so strong
But they aren't there when you're alone
You try to keep your composure
To keep your pain from exposure
Not to be viewed as vulnerable or weak
Being conscious of your expressions and the way you speak
Your heart can't fathom another break
So you keep it locked up
For your feelings sake
Know that it's okay to let your feelings pour out
Built this wall so they can't get in
Not realizing that you can't get out
Living and Learning
That's what life's all about
So live and learn
Until you find the best route

Be You

Be the best you that you can be
Dream so big
Beyond what you can see
Don't let anyone tell you
That something is impossible
Keep on pushing
Through the toughest of obstacles
Stop trying to fit in
When you were made to standout
Sometimes it is best
Not to follow the crowd
Be true to you
Not to anyone else
Make every effort to be
The greatest version of yourself.

Beautiful Black Woman

With her big full lips
And her thick round hips

She is a Beautiful Black Woman, Yes she is!

Those high cheekbones
And that milk chocolate skin
You can't help but notice
Her strength from within
The way she cleans and how she cooks
With her cover girl good looks

She is a Beautiful Black Woman, Yes she is!

Recognize her meekness
Not mistaken for weakness
Worth more than a medallion
With the stance of a stallion

She is a Beautiful Black Woman, Yes she is!

Just by her presence
She commands attention
Effortlessly confident
Not to mention

She is a Beautiful Black Woman, Yes she is!

That pride she can't hide
And her loyalty built of stone
Always there for support
The nature of a backbone

She is a Beautiful Black Woman, Yes she is!
Yes she is, a Beautiful Black Woman!

Seasons

As the seasons are changing
The wind is a breath of fresh air
Leave your past behind you
It is meant to stay there
Drop off all of your old leaves
Leave them where they lay
Sow good seeds in fertile soil
And Reap plentifully next may
Endure the cool nights like a willow tree
Bend and turn but don't break
You cannot expect to progress
If you never make and learn from mistakes.

A Special Someone

Someone who can see past your body
Into your mind and your soul
Someone whose warm touch melted your heart
Though it was so cold
Someone who is proud to have you by their side
Someone who feels blessed to walk with you
Takes pride in every stride
Someone who lifts you up
Whenever you are down
Someone who makes you smile
More often times than frown
Someone who is there to catch you
When you fall for them
Someone who is willing to be the tree
If you go out on a limb
Someone that's there to wipe your tears
Whose love grows stronger over the years
Someone who incites a passion
Deep from within
Someone who makes everyday feels like
When it first began
Someone who you can laugh with, Pray with or cry
Someone who constantly reminds you
Of how to love and why

Cowardly

Try to tear me down with your words
Because you're not so sure of yourself
Upset because I'm the real me
While you're content playing someone else
Staring in the mirror as you do each day
You barely recognize yourself
Busy pointing out everyone else's flaws
To avoid the fact that you need help
Using someone's self esteem
To push yourself up higher
Shows just how small you are
You're a counterfeit, phony liar!

Even When

Even when I'm in the shade

The sunshine still finds me

Even when I'm in the dark

My light is still shining

Even when I want to give up

My soul won't let me fall

I cannot hold my head down

I can only stand tall

Blessed

Think you're better than a person
Because of the things you have
If that's what you called blessed
Then you don't know the half

Are material things what validate you?
Then you don't know the truth
Ever felt like you just couldn't go on
And don't know how you made it through

Faith!

Seemed like no one around could understand
Until you felt his healing hand

Pray!

It's not so much as what you have
But more so who you are
The things I possess don't make me shine
Because I was born a star

You may be richer materialistically
But when it comes to character
You don't stand a chance
As long as I have Jesus by my side
I will always advance.

Own It

If you choose to keep quiet
Your voice will never be heard
Glide like an eagle
Not just a mere bird
Build your platform and own it
Take advantage of your moment
Until it is your time
Work hard, keep progressing
Go into overtime grind
Add substance to your name
Take over the game
Teach them to expect the best
In affiliation with you
Be your own biggest fan
And they will too!

Am I Wrong

Am I wrong for having big dreams?
Am I wrong for wanting nice things?
Am I wrong for setting the standards high?
Am I wrong for wanting more than just to get by?
Am I wrong for contradicting the stereotypes?
Am I wrong for not being caught up in the hype?
Am I wrong for being a heretic to the vast majority?
Am I wrong to choose gaining knowledge, as a top priority?
Am I wrong for progressing exceptionally well?
In areas where society expected me to fail
Am I wrong for breaking a family curse?
By graduating high school, marking a family's first
Am I wrong for wanting to see my brothers make it?
Somewhere other than the headlines of the news, catching cases
Am I wrong for wanting to see them leading the race?
Instead of leaving church in a hearse before their 21st birthday
Am I wrong to stand firm and be willing to fight?
Of course I'm not wrong I'm absolutely right!

Dear Society

Dear Society,
Was it designed for us to fail?
To sit back and watch the "dominant" race prevail
Why are we considered a minority?
When we make up the majority
Why are we ridiculed for this mentality?
When it was forced upon us, in reality
If knowledge is power
Why deprive a man of?
No wonder we tear each other down
Society has rarely shown us love
As far back as the days of Willie Lynch
He who left a very strong stench
Consciously using the word of the lord
As a powerful yet tormenting sword
To cut out a man's heart
And deny him a clean start
Mr. Lynch himself may be dead and gone
But hundreds of years later his legacy lives on

Is this the same society that said it was okay?
To treat a man as less than because of his dark skin
Instead of giving him a fair trial based on what's within.
To deliberately break a man from his natural state
Teach him not to be a man and take care of his family
But to cower away
Is this why we have so many single mother homes in black
communities today?
I know that it isn't completely your fault
After crawling for so long a person has to learn to walk
Not making excuses,
Just remembering the facts
Cheaters can only win for so long
Before the underdogs bounce back
The trials and tribulations gave us a tougher shell
After losing for so long we have no choice but to prevail.

L. was born in Atlanta, GA on July 22, 1987. She is the mother of two boys Shannon and Cameron. L. is a sophomore majoring in Secondary education at Atlanta metropolitan State College. She began writing poetry as a hobby in high school. She is deeply inspired by Maya Angelou, her favorite poet. L. aspires to become a national bestselling author and song writer in the near future. *Poetique Soul* is her first book of many to come. She hopes that her work will have the power to uplift, enlighten, and inspire every reader that has the opportunity read it. L. currently resides in Atlanta, GA.